TOWN

TOWN

Council:

Harold Abramowitz Amanda Ackerman Dorothy
Albertini Karen Leona Anderson Ana Božičević Mary
Cappello Kate Colby Ryan Daley Darcie Dennigan Claire
Donato Lisa Donovan Danielle Dreilinger Michael Tod
Edgerton Jenny Fowler Lori Fromowitz Elisa Gabbert
Kate Greenstreet Max Greenstreet Eli Halpern Matthew
Henriksen Erika Howsare Alexandra Hunter Brenda
Iijima Jackson Izzo Halvard Johnson Jennifer Karmin
Gillian Kiley Rauan Klassnik Jaimie Lea Konetchy Sam
Kusnetz Nora Jean Lange Hsiao-Shih Lee Dan Machlin
Sarah Madsen Douglas A. Martin James McShane
Jonathan Minton Jess Mynes Alistair Noon Kathleen
Ossip Michelle Brooks Parrish Katie Peterson Vanessa
Place Deborah Poe kathryn l. pringle Joan Retallack
Michael Robins Jennifer Romans Annie Schapira
Gabrielle Schapira **Kate Schapira** Rachel Schapira
Christopher Schmidt Zachary Schomburg Janaka Stucky
Dianne Timblin Chris Tonelli Tatiana Uhoch Adam Veal
Caroline Noble Whitbeck Lynn Xu Margaret Zamos-
Monteith Magdalena Zurawski

Factory School, 2010
Queens, New York

FOR JESS –
WITH THANKS &
ADMIRATION

TOWN
by Kate Schapira

Heretical Texts
Volume 5, Number 1

Factory School
Queens, NY, 2010

ISBN (paperback): 978-1-60001-065-1
ISBN (hardcover): 978-1-60001-066-8

Cover art by James McShane

Factory School is a learning and production collective engaged in action research, multiple-media arts, publishing and community service.

For more information, please visit factoryschool.org

Contents

CUSTOM / LAW   CONSTRUCTION / INFRASTRUCTURE

TOURISM

There is no such
thing as home. There's
no place

like home that
lingers not
surprisingly:

when Mrs. Lila
Corning was the head
of the Auxiliary
This town hosts a festival
It is an Autumn Leaf Festival
The Autumn Leaf Festival celebrates
the time of year when the town
leaves change

to brochures and flutter
and catch and pulp in the ordinary
street material
in some places

where the pavement is
thin
or cracked
the town leaves
room for ephemera.

The Auxiliary
Welcomes You.

TOURISM

TOPOGRAPHY

In the town there's a big lake
and in the big lake is a big I
sland. Can I name the island
and the lake? (Yes.) It's General's
Lake and Insoluble Island.
(Is it blue?) It's cobalt blue. (So
it's probably a very deep lake
then?) I guess it would be.

ANIMALS   CONSTRUCTION / INFRASTRUCTURE

TOURISM   MONUMENTS / RELICS

People used to say the only thing in town was to stand on the Smith Street overpass and watch all the cars going by. There are days we still feel this way when we walk on the overpass to and from work.

The town is the birthplace for those of us. In it, a dog death gutters and outcries. Conventional wisdom quickly gets out publicity to the effect that something gets born. This is a glottal bark that runs to the muzzle. A dog never lies sick in scaffolding. Dog death prefers heat risen from the ground, the elderly shopper's suddenly there on the grass, in the ghost of the scaffold's shadow. The bridge of the shopper's nose appears inflamed. Dog death becomes part of the next proclamation, ensuring that no one will hear of it, and is kept in municipal records for 25 years. Today dog death is a monument. •
Please support its daily upkeep, God bless.

From the dreamwall: Looking down and being sickened in a pleasurable way, like the mixing of stimuli at the birthplace, after a glottal bark series. Stomach turns to its animal nature for fun and relief as I walk up from the snarl, away from the sun.

CUSTOM / LAW   ANIMALS   CONSTRUCTION / INFRASTRUCTURE

CHANGES   TOPOGRAPHY

Birdhouses labeled the address with a half,
a quarter, three-quarters:

41 ½ April Street, 41 ¾ April Street
Chickadee, tufted titmouse and jay

used to be   all the streets
used to run through the center of town
a street called Elmcrest

Red clay bricks
but now it's called Montana
years from now we'll call
it Crescent Drive
bristling with saplings
as the moon does

the town council's
scooters drawn up at the blocks
below the height of the wall
into their measured spaces.

The official mallard duck
is often seen preening on
General's Lake
and on duck stamps   all
the streets are one-way

CONSTRUCTION / INFRASTRUCTURE
HAUNTINGS   COMMERCE / CURRENCY

CHANGES   TOPOGRAPHY

Toward the end of the great shipping days when movies
made about trains proliferated more than trains, old men moved
uphill from the sea and depleted the local timber.
Their widows' walks looked out on burnt-looking mountains
at best   their ghosts are collectors of
pride, whose pride in accumulation and drift, and building
widows' walks, white. Where do they come in?

CONSTRUCTION / INFRASTRUCTURE

CONTRADICTIONS   HAUNTINGS   COMMERCE / CURRENCY

DISASTER

CHANGES

Well, I think this town should revolve around the
suburbs which surround it.

The homes in this town are mostly very small
cottages. It was doing great financially a couple
decades ago because people bought summer
homes and time-shares there.

These suburbs are composed of neighborhoods,
streets lined with so many trees that a tunnel is
seemingly formed. The fathers drive from their
homes

but once the factory fire destroyed the town
economy during the winter months, many of the
locals couldn't afford their mortgages and moved
out of their remote and larger houses,

and either go to work in the town or in the city,
which is much farther from these suburbs.

and moved full-time into the tiny little cottages
once intended for only short-term use. This
resulted in property values going down; eventually
even the nice homes in town were available for
Section 8.

The town and suburbs are ruled by where the fathers
work. The mothers and wives act accordingly and
raise thirsty children respectively,

> Many claim with a hint of complete pride that their
> old houses are haunted—by a sea captain or teen
> suicide ...

the restaurant's children facing the factory's
children, reflected in nothing, protective
discoloration ...

FROM THE DREAMWALL: I dreamed there was a city to be our double star, between us dry wilds and alpine meadows. To get there I drove down a long green tunnel of fortune forever. Dust went before me and behind me. I knew somehow this was a dream of the future. Plural sounds came. I was part of a thundering herd that stopped and marked with its cheek glands, the whole car became a body, wallowing motion. I knew I had to be somewhere.

CONSTRUCTION / INFRASTRUCTURE

FOOD   CONTRADICTIONS

CHANGES   PLUMBING   TOPOGRAPHY

Town was built next to the river. Later, the railroad came. The planners didn't see fit to curve over to town, but instead passed seven miles to the east—at which point about half the residents decided to move there, building around the train station. That second town is our town, built around the railroad lines, at the junction of two railroad lines that have been competing very bitterly with each other since the 1880s that grew up around the railroad lines, the bitter coal years, the corncob riots.

Revisiting the original town of this, contradiction seemed to have melted. The railroad our old town was built around was the river. The planners didn't see fit to curve over. The train station waved a dusty hand at the river, the old town, the changing nature of needs, and started running water. The river didn't even see the old town in the street.

Overlap apologetically, one step wet, the next dry. Revisit the heat belt, shaking brownfield between track and track, nothing will grow / or / plants separate themselves from the mulch of dung and ash / and / are firmly pulled by auxiliary fingers / maybe here impossibility enters the taut border.

CONSTRUCTION / INFRASTRUCTURE

CONTRADICTIONS   HAUNTINGS

PLUMBING

never a cruel moment, this month
in the overlaid   gingerbread
flaking

            what's it named after
waiting for your Section
8 months later partakes
of the very strict
imaginary and the real

does the toilet   do the lights
walking through the old summer turning
singing wordlessly   tunelessly haunted
by your own   house

            can you help me
figure out if this is sad or not

CONSTRUCTION / INFRASTRUCTURE

FOOD   COMMERCE / CURRENCY

PLUMBING

Dye from the corduroy factory ran and marked the clothes of
factory workers whose noses, lint-starched, caked and dried and
never ran. Their saliva was hard put to it.

Fish processing brings home the search for running water to the
albugineous surfaces of "before" versions, the heaviest drinkers,
freezers, the odor a signpost erected before the town had signs.

Orange groves shine with ordinance and dust with work, and are
heavy. You wouldn't believe how heavy but they do grow. Do sigh
from a distance, their motions just as repetitive, canals and sprayers
run to them from the lake, from the river, across the plain.

The railroad comes close enough, loads shipping containers onto
flat car beds, cans, crates, pallets, all steeply, all stately. We are
trying to find a new identity. Now comes videophone technology.
For this, the trains have tiny cars.

CONSTRUCTION / INFRASTRUCTURE
CONTRADICTIONS

PLUMBING   TOPOGRAPHY

In our recent past we were dry, overrun
but not run down by   diviners in search of running
          water.

There's a dam where couples go to hang out on first dates. Hand
down the pants while standing type thing   farms at our
furthest   lovers' fertile water lane.
In our town, as the water stands,

the avenues are of water. Can't call them lagoons, barely nine
inches over worn brown
and gray cobbles of the narrows in the northern
taken from the crumbling stone silos of defunct boundaries,
throwing the wheels of scooters, skateboards, bikes. Tufts of fur
taken alive on them.

Used to be all the streets were made of red clay bricks. In time
these were paved over with ordinary street material

Farms at our furthest   nosed coarsely up through
in some places where perception is thin
or cracked

          by the pond or General's Lake
seven miles from the river
as the level of the nearby sea
has risen to squirm over the surface   streets
          cross them.

COMMERCE / CURRENCY

DISASTER
CHANGES

This town is the birthplace.
Change is inevitable. A minister cites
Ecclesiastes. Townspeople riot

quietly, in their houses, by videophone.

(The videophone riots of the year
2021 coincided with the death
of the last witness, who never told
anyone he was there at the time.

He died at 99 after years
on a diet of secret currency,
soup from the Coffee-Lunch, butter,
margarine, and nutritional yeast.

From his brownfield grave
hybridized violets sprang.)

CUSTOM / LAW
CONTRADICTIONS

EDUCATION

Everyone sings once a day: it's not required, just expected.
Presently, no songs in town, but everyone sings anyway. Just not
songs waver and tremble and rise, nasal or chesty at tasks—on the
way to the shrink's office—in between bites of money.

At Crooked Places Made Straight Christian Academy students
sing tremulous just not hymns across the giddy divide of changing
voices about the diseases men gained from congress with sheep,
policed if their harmonies rub too close. They learn tri-tones, the
devil's intervals. Scare the squirrels, peer at each other.

Greater harmonies of adults mingle with scooter exhaust and the
fish-processing whistle.

Since there's no preschool, the littlest kids sing in total absorption,
unsmacked unless they accidentally hit on an actual song. Control
isn't always right, it's whispered firmly, custom isn't always subtle.
Send that child out into town knowing what, unwavering.

In the center of town, a factory: dull cement with corncob windows. No one sees in, no one out. Corncob in; corncob out. Corncob the center of town, its field of ears and maze and pole and shucking. Corncobs deliver the factory. Corncob repurposes 1) butter, 2) margarine, 3) nutritional yeast. The corncob statue olfactory, metal at its core? Corncob out and upward to the sky, symbolizing 1) death, 2) the town's minister, and 3) a regime of power at the forefront of the Corncob Revolution of the mid-1850s.

Under 100 years later, the council built a shelter below Main Street to protect the dairy cows from the stress and noise of air raids. Because it was little used, they converted it to an underground storage tank for milk. The rumbling of traffic slowly turned the milk into cream, then butter. So we may or may not have 900 square feet of possibly rancid butter under Main Street. Everyone's afraid to go down and check it out; in front of the firehouse, we dare each other to take a big whiff, tag the statue, skate around the factory counterclockwise. Main runs parallel to Montana, the traffic circles, big ugly fountain, graves and clapboard.

Brick and green lawns bright as an eyesore. Today's town council scoots to work over mysteries, bridging shallow water avenues with worn brick ease. No one believes in public art; corncob just the same. Silage is a lonely business.

CONTRADICTIONS   HAUNTINGS

DISASTER   MONUMENTS / RELICS

PLUMBING

—Once a year, survivors gather at the old water
pump where someone's erected a plaque that
reads "Rest in Peace"

without names or dates   Not surprisingly
the field of psychoanalysis is booming   with girl ghosts

the buildings burned   the old Girl Scout
20 years ago   the factory in 1984
backed by last year's natural disaster simultaneously
never caught and never happening   ghost
memory syndrome   seemingly
happy couples and triples bereaved, survival
floating in the air   more about this later

CONSTRUCTION / INFRASTRUCTURE

FOOD   CONTRADICTIONS   COMMERCE / CURRENCY

Money is a building block.

The town uses food. This has *always*
been the case: Instead of banks, a food
storage warehouse. Instead of wallets,

> Every two weeks when men and women take their
> paychecks and cash them at the bank. They don't
> deposit the money but begin to chew it.

brown paper bags. A jar of tomatoes is
worth less than a bunch of fresh carrots,
but more than a pound of dried beans.

> Swallowing is considered wasteful;

The key to freshness is value, or distance from
source. Everyone chews their currency but

> when each bill is good and chewed, they spit it
> onto a crepe griddle where it's smoothed and
> heated. After this material (cotton, actually)
> emerges it is often more pliable cud, later shaped
> and layered into bricks, from which houses may be
> made:

the divide is powerful and refined.

in the mortgage lines they say, "I'm paying for my
house with houses." Locals who can't maintain
their mortgages with chewed cud money moved
into the old food-economy cottages.

Truckloads of new money enter town.
No cornfields near, just the corncob
factory, and gardens. In the mortgage
lines the bewildered hold

their arms stiffly full: beets,
translucent onions, sound of beans in paper like a hailstorm,
reflected glow of hope that holds from the future, without botulism
or foreclosure / take out a kimchee loan on the well-developed jaw
muscles of the rich and be turned away staggering home this time
with all the wealth of the world

summer kitchen tacked onto the back of the cottage intended for
short-term use fragile currency rotting antique stores closing

FOOD   COMMERCE / CURRENCY

        TOURISM

(Mrs. Bodega)

Pallets of paper turned and wrapped
square as a jaw facing leaving /
cornered as impeccable / polite to
the social worker with the small-
town counter manners / what to do
for an anemone / what to do for anyone
known for accepting both kinds /
the flowers are beautiful, but cold
and bitter displays of gladioli, dyed
carnations, tight roses / sandwiches
in plastic months / everything is
stiff except the newspapers

(I always wonder about her. She
never seems happy.)

Questions of tear ducts just   (Mrs. Newsstand)
complicate her friendships   (Mrs. Corner Store)

keeps a bootleg crepe griddle in
the back / on payday takes a smaller
cut than the official vendors / the
material may be flawed / some go

quickly / they don't care / they think
it's worth it / with uneven heat

(Everyone recognizes her value.
You will probably see her when you stay.)

FROM THE DREAMWALL: We were hanging a man from the shadow of the hanging tree. It was like a picnic, with children. I told my husbands, "Children shouldn't see this." His shadow bulged out, but there was no sound. The tree wavered like when a cloud crosses. People said they were cleaning up the town, but I didn't do anything to stop them. Times were different then, in my dream. People meeting who hadn't met for years, it was like a party, kissing, wrestling, their backs to the tree.

CUSTOM / LAW
FOOD   HAUNTINGS
                        TOURISM
CHANGES

Its recent past was a dry town. Now politically
split between those who wish it
still was and those we drink heavily, their numb
ash sinking
to the bottom
of our water

Filter the bathtub liquor, take the pepper
to the bottom

mmmm—that's sediment
you take with
you, like the white
of an eye or egg, white-
colored, spermy,

(haunted. We had buried our heartache in souvenirs,
American-made crates, berries
pliable like
funnel cakes

The dead came back to
remind us what was gone.
There was a fire
also. So
that didn't help)

in the local soda.

Mothers and fathers work
at the corduroy factory.
Cotton fluff like flocking on them.
They're their children's toys, the
mothers and fathers, and mothers
and mothers and fathers, and fathers
and fathers and mothers. Fluff settles
on everything, thickens everything,
brown and maroon, "Creamate" in

company coffee thickening the break
room. Working accordingly
and respectively, they don't
keep any of it, except in their lungs
it lies in heaps the colors of bruises:
maroon, dark brown, tan, olive
green, cloudy blue, lavender.
Fathers, some of whom are mothers,
drive from their homes, drive back

to their homes under ghosts of future
trees and grown children, their
colors made redundant by
darkness and sodium vapor. The factory
exists as a ghost of motes in
air, paralleled, particulate,
collapsing, illuminated. The fire
of 1984 erected in the winter months
with thirteen father and mother

survivors spun out. Cotton lint went
up like snow. The factory's gone

and there, drifting in and out of sun.
Everything—people, patterns—went
along where only fire is made
becoming what it is and isn't
about the ghosts in the factory
when they move themselves busily,
sent up, still flecked and working.

CONTRADICTIONS   HAUNTINGS

DISASTER   EDUCATION

The difficulty of the Kingdom
of Heaven is to coexist, not to exist.
It must rise up like a mutation. It might not
look at all like you when it's born. Crooked
Places Made Straight Christian Academy

bountifully founded
opens its peeling doors still reeling
students a (careful Bible) trip
thumping away with round
wrists and tight
hair to the dam, to the wrecked haunted Girl
Scout building where
they write their names
on cinderblocks where
they kiss what they've heard of
in pity and terror where
one did big violence to
another, any other, under
ministerial breath like
a cloud of oily fog.

The ghost of a chance to be embraced by part of love leading
to reservation, simultaneous combustion. Looking to either side
is this a potential lover or murderer. These can coexist until
the box of the body opens, if you admit it. The town is where.

Explain what you've never understood: how to be a child victim.
This is what we learn in school, but don't repeat.

FROM THE DREAMWALL: I dreamed Geena and I were messing around on the leaf pile. Then I had a baby. The baby was in a clear plastic bubble, like my stomach was a clear plastic bubble, like a museum case. The baby was the reincarnation of a ghost girl but it was a boy, covered with this white gunk and black fur. Geena said lots of babies have that but I knew mine was different. Everybody brought oranges to the wedding.

ANIMALS

CONTRADICTIONS   HAUNTINGS

CHANGES

strange beasts drift through the town, grazing

the beasts can be seasonal
they cannot possibly be human

watering at the canals, gazing
longingly at Insoluble Island

they just go around stepping in
all the houses and all the museums

there's no history now where
anyone can live, and now nothing

is left, it's just a hole in
the stomach of the world

where everything is hungry—
a kind of desert, matchstick

ruins, shattered cases,
tattered proclamations, terra

cotta fragments of a terrace the color
of orange peels in burned-

out weeds and ashes
spreading like

the awkward decision not
to remember soft spotted

coats, cud-chewing, migrating
strands of saliva—

without this, people line
up at the fish-processing plant, the factory

(ghostly) and the bank, the hanging
tree (mythical) and the animals

overlap them with piles of
herbivorous droppings the size

of houses and museums. The historical
society has a terrible time,

the present holds the town for ransom,
most of the beasts have horns

—the minute it becomes the past
you can't prepare for it or protect it.

CUSTOM / LAW
                CONTRADICTIONS   HAUNTINGS
                        TOURISM   MONUMENTS / RELICS   EDUCATION

The Crooked Places Made
Straight Christian Academy
sophomore class takes a
trip to the museum. They
praise cataloguing and stick-
toitiveness. They don't
touch the new cases with
sticky bad hands. *We're*

constant in danger, lessening than relics, much more than dogs, much
much much more than that bad mystery that sticks us together. Sexual
identity fluid. Is a threat. Our heads must be counted we angry-groined
potentials, the serial mystery never caught, reeling from body to body.
Embody a dead thing cased in the mud of the lake. Mercy on fewer of us.
Heaven protect us. In
the exuberance between us
Cases are necessary

evils required to protect
objects from dust and the
fingers of visitors. The less
obtrusive the better, but since
they cannot be altogether
inconspicuous, they should be
tasteful. A suitable case is a
setting for its contents
as well as a protection, *body*

as temple, not as dam where all detritus ferments our double and triple education, sculpture that comes alive or loose, brushes past us with fear. Those fluid people over there are here, they marry in haste, foamy and smiling we stay in after dark. We are particular. The dam brushes against a spill of threat at the same time,

the same time.
We get in line.

CUSTOM / LAW

FOOD   CONTRADICTIONS   HAUNTINGS

MONUMENTS / RELICS   EDUCATION

CHANGES

The oak transplanted to become
the hanging tree since town had been assigned
an infamously stern judge moved to the site
appearing quite strong for its size and presumed
youth, a chinquapin oak—which are typically tall,
sturdy. As it turned out this tree was a dwarf
variety. It took quite a while to realize it would never be
suitable. By that time the judge himself had died
slipping from the roof of his home while stargazing.

Without the judge there was neither urgency
nor a municipal work order so the tree
was never replaced. In time it stood as a town
symbol appearing in the emblem of the historical
society housed in the courthouse building.
Later it was cut down by a new guy
who mistook it for a stunted elm despite
the historical society's best efforts,

the fables of outlaws and bandits meeting
their end on the lawn outside the courthouse.
Some of us are nostalgic for the future
some look forward to gossip. The silk of new grass
catches on everything, on the hanging
version of history, the future in trees,
banking on it. Today there's a proclamation.
Last week, a proclamation. We sit
in the Coffee-Lunch. Watch the courthouse:
each new law ushers in a flag. The Mayor's
a blur, a brass band plays.

In front of the courthouse real picnickers
overlap the feet of notional convicts
dangling. Nothing dimming the sun on
their lapel ribbons, couples and triples coo.
The river is low and far away. The orange
groves march to it. No one complains.
No single bill regarding schools although
the students use each other for fuel.

Any floodwaters must be earlier,
be powerful or psychosomatic, between
the old town and the new bodies
bloating on dry land in sympathy,

canals filling, spilling—wet sidewalks is all—
down the cheeks of streets, children,
who have no memory, are marching steadily.
                              If, in an earlier
infatuation, we'd been in a race with time,
now we live as though time will never
run out, not now, not ever, for us or on us.

CUSTOM / LAW
FOOD

CHANGES

A family moved into a house on a quiet street. Once they were
unpacked they evoked all their neighbors' doors to invite them
over for a watermelon margarita block party. The night of the house
only two old women came. As the second entered and was greeted
by the couple she shook hands with the other. Both women were
widowed. Their houses sat next to each other and each had lived in
her own since just after a young marriage. On this night they were
introduced.

Hospitality holds its breath as the mixture delivers. Both have
grown old and human. To say, "We're both old," that age happens
not to the other but both, to be part of both in town, to remember
the houses they moved from dwindling in memory, becoming
matchstick, streets spreading and tiring easily, evening melting
in cautious red sips. They were about the changes of which other
neighbors were a part, sitting as they'd been taught, two women
spreading and diffusing to reenter matter, like soaked gauze,
quietly into the fiber of town as streetlights marked out the web of
veins filled with isotopes moving weakly.

The couple whose house it was told everyone how sweet it was
from the outside, quick coming to tongue, loosening flavor. The
sunset looked like a lake of watermelon margaritas.

FOOD

TOURISM

CHANGES

She was the heroine. He was the organist
and town drunk. The graveyard
where she would've been buried
is behind the church, white clapboard.
The terrace is salvaged orange

and gray bricks and pale-brown
of folding, former money. He escaped
liver failure, jake-leg in the dry years,
but he's deaf now. Needs looking after.
She's fat and hard to move. The thumbnail
on her peeling hand is yellow.

The organ's tattered bellows
have mice and bats in their leather,
old purses of bodies. In a way

they wish they felt better.
In a way it's peaceful.
They have a lot to remember.
The organ wheezes like a
disappointed suitor. They both tell
strangers the stories he can't hear:

what does it mean to say, *natural.*
What does it mean to say, *until.*

CUSTOM / LAW   CONSTRUCTION / INFRASTRUCTURE
FOOD   HAUNTINGS   COMMERCE / CURRENCY
        TOURISM

From a brochure: *Care to join the bread parade? Follow the city council on a cavalcade of scooters. The Mayor trails ribbons (supplied by the Auxiliary), then the ghosts, bovine and human, then the children too young for school, scattering. Everyone else is at work, or wishing they were at work, or can't move well. The bread is warm—baked in the tender—and round with a hard crust. The firemen throw it from open, more than adequate doors, to the ceremonial mob, while freightmen load up the boxcars with practiced heaves. It's as if the bread were distracting the crowd while the real work got done. It's as if its rising odor were a tremendous show that didn't matter, an exclusive offer where everything works smoothly and everyone's covered in coal smoke, including the teeth. Clutching the blackened bread, they return, dismantling their ribbons.*

CUSTOM / LAW   ANIMALS
      CONTRADICTIONS
         TOURISM   MONUMENTS / RELICS
CHANGES

The alligators carry candles on their backs for lights in the parade.

        The ringleader squirrel has a rat tail.

Trimmed paths lead alligators and followers from the air.

        The march is nearly overgrown.

The gazebo sparkles with bandleaders.

        The bonfire has already spread.

To walk is the pleasure of flowers and shouting at night.

        Entire thing coated in a very thick tangle
        of ivy and weeds.

The alligator parade is the new-clothes event.

        The nests in the topiary stink.

In the teeming profusion of summer lacewings file,

Nobody ever gets married here.

street games gather like mist around the island.

Dealers, wannabe gangsters, sulky
breakers, bad elements,

Fingernail moon covers everybody home,

hungry ghosts, that fine-grained black dirt
we know so well glitters with glass.

from miles around to the town's many gates.

Lowlives, loveliness, the low lights.

CUSTOM / LAW
      CONTRADICTIONS
DISASTER   MONUMENTS / RELICS
CHANGES

Town says *always* with perfect confidence, sighs when it sees the large wax seal, re-elects the Mayor way before the mall and any revitalization art projects began. There's a place in the park for a statue but there's never (as far as anyone can remember) been a statue there /
           there's a statue   a placard   an honor which the firemen are pretty good about keeping clean, hands-on, wavering, declining, never discussing the past. Some flickers above the Mayor's head, a fuzzy change. He is here /
                       heard remotely, in a ribbon of bad signal, never changing /
                     changing in number, in water, in fire, in the bodies pulled from these.

ANIMALS

HAUNTINGS   COMMERCE / CURRENCY

CHANGES

Videophone magnates blink and flash, their sharp
outlines thinking of being history.
The town will believe anything in a picture.
They'll believe abbreviated words skittering over
the top layers of faces like cuttlefish.
They'll lift special little dogs to get them into the image too.

Older industries tessellate out.
What is a ghost?
A set of dust with light on it.
An accident.
A smear, a blunder ...

Shelter beyond the door
Value furnishes all our
images
m o t i o n l e s s

relying on dim gleams

Where the image freezes, the voice keeps chewing
industriously, truly economically.
These windows are made of pure future pain.
The progress that makes them brings tears to our eyes.

ANIMALS

FOOD   CONTRADICTIONS   HAUNTINGS

After a glottal bark series
the last witness can just about
chew scrambled eggs
and eat fish soup, which
the one-legged cook—nephew's
husband?—makes for him
without being asked. The bowl
seems full of dark portents,
murky, mosaic, viral. He taps
Creamate into his free refill.
He couldn't possibly be seeing her.
He couldn't have seen her then.

That nephew steps and stomps
the counter muffling
his deckside lurch. Make you
seasick just to see him.
They caught her out at
the border, out past
curfew, with the bat sounds.
Crooked Places Made Straight
Christian Academy has just let
out and the kids are screaming,
making slurs, placing French fries
in each other's hair out of love.
Time trapped her. She never got
this far. She can't be among them
differently then. Nephew
stumps over and refills him.
His apron is a firetrap. In this

town you can die by fire or water
or hold yourself for her fate,
he keeps quiet, the mallards
of imperfect understanding rest
in his yard like the town's great seal.
He can see her now. He can't
be seeing her here.

FROM THE DREAMWALL: I dreamed another town that I reached via a little two-car train, carrying my leather grip. Evergreens and ochre rocks, pastel three-story buildings and a handicraft market in a limestone cave series. Artists gathered on dark wood floors with melting varnish to seriously converse and long for each other. Everyone there was young for some reason, or maybe I just couldn't see the old people very well. This town had a few things in common with other towns, it was haunted by the expectation of town, but town is permanent. I spent most of my time in the dream in the caves, looking for someone. The town consists of two steps: being unable to imagine anything but what's already happened, and suiting your imagination to what you couldn't have imagined before. This is what keeps the town a town and the dream a dream: the assumption that humans will only be replaced by other humans, the difficulty of finding anyone over the sound of the sea. We return to the town in dreams. It's our civic duty.

ANIMALS   CONSTRUCTION / INFRASTRUCTURE

FOOD   CONTRADICTIONS   HAUNTINGS

MONUMENTS / RELICS

CHANGES

Defunct farms at the northern boundary brought their cows to town streets when the bombs started to declare themselves in other places. Cows gave nervous milk underground as aforesaid until the war was over, sour.

Sock-hops, Valium use, the '60s, disco, and Wham! emptied the farms. Herds died, were sold, or ambled. A real cow might seem to be a ghost cow. Even waiting to feel its breath or see if flies went to it, we couldn't be sure. Meanwhile the substance of our success after corn and before videophones turned into cream, then butter, then rancid possibility.

Some say the cows conceived. Now they get to keep their milk for their strange, horned or scaled infants, soft as lint. We keep our distance. Their look of mild surprise never changes to longing.

FOOD CONTRADICTIONS COMMERCE / CURRENCY
TOURISM
CHANGES

Now the smells under the red roof have changed. Delhi: isn't that
the name of a town? Flavor on the air has changed, staining fingers
with an autumn leaf stain. A kind of desert, where everything is
hungry for American grease.

Town's thriving, revolving around. Who says things—who says
things are fine? Did they stop for a paper cone of pakora on their
way downhill? Where do they return to—to buildings smaller than
their feet? Is it really a problem of scale? You can sit in any ruins, in
ruins of any size, like the white of an eye.

When did they know it? Came they to eat, first at the Roy
Rogers, then at the Delhi Express, with delicate fingertips?
Cautious, nonlocal fingertips? I won't comment on their peristaltic
proclivities, a stereotype of swamps and tender musings.

The skin of a brown first. We said the town was running downhill.
Our white like that of an eye. But we contains them now, or they
discolor we, surely the town has a threat, surely its form is its
nature.

A rogue element. We're not all like this.

CUSTOM / LAW
                CONTRADICTIONS   HAUNTINGS   COMMERCE / CURRENCY

CHANGES   PLUMBING   TOPOGRAPHY

Insoluble Island / a hideout no one can get to / see the past with
nimble / dancing on
the air above it

Sometimes in the town, intentions change, or result

in former lives running / but downhill, to water, in / search of water,
messengers only / to water / divinely / that this was / wherever / the
avenues of water ran from was inexhaustibly former / money rinsing
from this / disintegration / chewed and spat out and spreading,
blanketing and growing / counterintuitive to models / the level of
the sea is rising / growth models growth as that which runs uphill /
which creeps / seas, the old river bend, General's / they don't need
to *find* / water / is easy to find but can't be handled / can't make
profusion flourish

                                        on its own
                                        on the surface of

sight / no one uses pronouns / names, choices and mills / gestures
of the head / plumage mixed with hair / only expressing / timidity /
but less in the way of spooking

                                        the local government
                                        has

located money away
from massive models of urban decay / what is it that springs / you
know / you tell me / if we live that long

MONUMENTS / RELICS   EDUCATION
CHANGES

On the statue of
Erik Chase's chest
the Superman logo,

the boxy peel of kids away
from Crooked
Places Made Straight's

pistachio-colored
patina
the grass

of love or
hatred: "Geena
is a liar," "Juggalo
4 Lyfe," hearts
and projections local

hero sculpted in
his gear, the broad
back of his coat a
slate on which

to inscribe the town
children who've been
born since, sad

boxwoods, their
own opportunities,
popularities, intimating
the tribe of

the town where
nothing and no
one will save them.

Firemen aren't looking.
They're looking for fires.
Being young is
a disaster but

not the natural
disaster everyone
leans against the day.
Town will
cough them up
like an impurity

or retain them.
They look
through their bodies

as half-walled over-
growth
with envy.

FROM THE DREAMWALL: I dreamed I smashed all the dishes, all the jars. I stood at the factory fire and threw handfuls of corn into it, from the blackness outside it. By the time it's a story there will be no one to tell it. Mild eyes will make no distinction. Trees and the remnants of houses will grow up through the streets. It's too late not to think about it. Once the trail roared through with its long golden mane in the dew-soaked morning. War never came here, but change came to thicken the water, to the spheres of flesh inside, tiny possibilities. Who dreams they give birth to the town's tree-heavy future? Write your dream underneath mine.

FROM THE DREAMWALL: Sometimes I don't think laws are so bad.

CHANGES

The beast had a comforting
yogurt smell but didn't want her
to touch its fur. It made some sounds
as it moved away and she thought
it was trying to talk to her or giving
her a sign, so she made sounds back,
its next sounds she made, it's not always easy
to hear how these things spread. Imagination
stops at the burnt edge of grass. About
ten months later she gave birth to a kid
who had a little something, at
first they thought it was chemicals from
her work at the videophone plant, but
meanwhile plants at the edges were growing
like crazy, insects were trying to pollinate
each other. Someone tried planting an orange
seedling but it wasn't reliable, it wasn't
even safe ... people started talking to each
other in versions of the sounds, but you
could never be sure, gestures came
into it, there were some fights ... police
were everywhere, but policing was a more
relative item, at the molecular level.
Ash and dung mixed to form a fertile crescent
rocked with glottal barks and singing not
songs. Many of the things humans wanted
to relate became impossible: she couldn't
say *Did you click aah today?* only *Re click aah
is there*, so we stopped doing those human
things. Some of us. Some of them. The oranges
came up toxic. It wasn't reasonable.
She gave a great hoarse cry.

CUSTOM / LAW   CONSTRUCTION / INFRASTRUCTURE
FOOD   CONTRADICTIONS
                         MONUMENTS / RELICS
          PLUMBING

Over by the half-rotten gazebo there's a triple wedding going
defiantly on, bedraggledly there's the trail of litter they abandon,
raided by squirrels. Guests pound their Bibles vigorously when
the triple kisses, gracefully, like they practiced, without their noses
getting in the way. In the past the train would've brought them
orchids that morning, fountains would've been running, ugly,
transfigured with curtains of water piped up through the gates.
This is for the day: they walk to the outskirts all in arm through the
remaining gate, garlanded with pearly crowns of garlic skins and
pea pods,

and although aunts and uncles may go home and feel smug about
their own, brief or long-lasting, glandular or convenient, one will
make the thin tea, one will take the trash out to form a growing
shadow obscuring the moon, one will put well-chewed money on
the table,

one will cross the names out of the Bible. The statue erected for
the wedding out of corncobs and garlic skins will slough away
over the days until the squirrels take care of it. Contradict a triple
marriage: incredulity, simultaneity and fact. A dubious pact with the
present can't be, but it is, we're telling you, before the language of
vows becomes corrupt or we refuse to acknowledge it,

oh sweetness.

After years scorning the food economy, the last witness can no longer chew his pension. Shreds, drool, fall. Birds flock around the numbered birdhouses like souvenirs. Peck at what he's left around his helpless feet.

She's a hole in the stomach of his memory. She's become *his* ghost. No one knows how she died. No one knows he was there. Other people see her as a bluish or greenish glow—she doesn't seem tied to a place, or repulsive, but looks like she needs sleep. Sometimes her outline crumbles like a border. Sometimes his throat fills with her bones. He makes sounds like the beasts, like the birds. The one-legged cook gets ready to follow the choking instructions on the wall.

FROM THE DREAMWALL: I'm the keeper of information. People blurt their stories to me and never come back, leaving strings of lake perch or bags of dried beans—I don't take cud money. It's the videophones, they wail, the videophones are stealing our identities—and it's true their faces look a little vague, or worn like lake stones or like the resolution is patches of painter's color. Tell me about yourself, I said, I'll keep it for you a little at a time, but more and more of their faces glitter oddly, blandly, the texture of scales. Leave it with me, I say, but they never come back for it. I put the beans in water to soak, fry the fish and eat them slowly in what seems like my kitchen but every handle's the wrong shape.

ANIMALS

FOOD   COMMERCE / CURRENCY

CHANGES

Walk to the newsstand with your
glowing eyes: tomatoes came
up early this year. Her mouth's
the surface of the lake. Take
a paper and some change. You
heard about the animals over
on Crescent Drive? She
dumps three bulbs and a paper
into your palm. You look at
your palm. She says, "All
our grandparents were former people."

ANIMALS

CHANGES   TOPOGRAPHY

In the future, town will have trees come up through bricks and
cobbles siding them over ghosts by knitting their bones *rra click*
dense intractable web of cracked *click all* textures in the trees or
future, spoiled wheels and sparrows, crows, peaceful macrofauna,
fertilizing shade inhabiting the mouth of the lake *crr hlaa* there's
no choice, in the future this town will be the past of a municipal
planting overturning handmade elements with its rise, pouchy
and swelling trunks, cheeks *lle click click lle* trapping and censoring
water. No one to *click ala*, surprise is *rra* slow, don't hold your breath
for it, for drama we need humans pawned and appealed to, blamed.

ANIMALS
CONTRADICTIONS
TOURISM
CHANGES

Upon discovery we do what we've always: assimilate
change in long ropy strands

slowly revolving us like muscles: the daily round
circles the fountain trickling the line of least

heat: If you come to look at us what us is it.
What we insisting has been scaled all along

changing the route around the long-lashed side-eye we assign
history dangling caked from the hair under our tails

Every day is April, April
Every animal is a fool

We lean against our soft sides where the multi-limbs attach
We herd: we exclude: we are included.

FROM THE DREAMWALL: She smiled at me and told me to put it to rest. She was glad I could see her. She said, "Tell them," or maybe, "You don't need to tell them." She had undergone mouthparts, but I wasn't disgusted or afraid, I didn't have to wash her off.

FROM THE DREAMWALL: I dreamed he came back, but his hooves were full of orchids. He came down from the mountains. I didn't want to see him. I told him to go. He made those sounds, the ones they make. He walked through the town, his turds glittered. I found myself trying to make the sounds back, so he would understand that I wanted him to leave. He walked into the sea.

About Town

This is how TOWN began:

Hey everyone,
I'm making a town. Right now it's in my head. Eventually it'll be in
a book—many of you are familiar with the little books I make.
What I'd like you to do is tell me one thing about this town's past or
present. You don't have to think about it too hard. Just type it in and
send it to me. May I suggest that you do it sooner rather than later,
for busyness and memory reasons. I'll use anything I get before April
Fool's day.
Write to send me your contribution to the town or to ask questions.
Municipally,
Kate Schapira

As information about the town came in from friends, relations and acquaintances (some of whom are working writers, others not), some of it started to contradict itself (some pieces contradicted others), and since I'd decided that everything people told me about the town was true, I had to revisit my ideas about consensus: how do contradictions mutually and simultaneously exist and what gravity do they exert on one another, without one erasing or swallowing the other?

I also began to sort contributions into a number of notional bins or committees, and you can see those at the beginning of each poem, categorizing, overlapping, bounding and spilling. Things seem more important than they are, and vice versa. Things change in town; town changes. What kind of 'we' statements can the town make and still be true / without having to be true?

The original plan was in fact to make a chapbook edition, but while working on the project I submitted TOWN to Factory School and we decided to present it this way.

This is the town my contributors and I made. With the same set of contributions you could found your own town—any number of towns. The question is not whether we live differently in the same world, but how.

FACTORY SCHOOL
Heretical Texts Series

factoryschool.org/ht
distributed by spdbooks.org